To share her

love of reading. . .

a gift from

**Martha  Huckins,**

Franklin's former librarian

## Ocean Life

# Jellyfish

## By Lloyd G. Douglas

Children's Press®
A Division of Scholastic Inc.
New York / Toronto / London / Auckland / Sydney
Mexico City / New Delhi / Hong Kong
Danbury, Connecticut

Photo Credits: Cover © John Warden/Getty Images; p. 5 © Sissie Brimberg/National Geographic/ Getty Images; p. 7 © Fred Bavendam/Minden Pictures; p. 9 © Robert Huberman/SuperStock, Inc.; p. 11 © Stuart & Cynthia Pernick/SuperStock, Inc.; p. 13 © Robert Yin/Corbis; pp. 15, 21 © Royalty-Free/Corbis; p. 17 © Stuart Westmorland/Corbis; p. 19 © Ann & Rob Simpson

Contributing Editor: Shira Laskin
Book Design: Elana Davidian

Library of Congress Cataloging-in-Publication Data

Douglas, Lloyd G.
    Jellyfish / by Lloyd G. Douglas.
    p. cm. — (Ocean life)
    Includes index.
    ISBN 0-516-25025-6 (lib. bdg.) — ISBN 0-516-23738-1 (pbk.)
    1. Jellyfishes—Juvenile literature. I. Title.

    QL377.S4D68 2005
    593.5'3—dc22
                                                    2004010110

# Contents

1 Jellyfish     4

2 Tentacles     12

3 Different Jellyfish     14

4 New Words     22

5 To Find Out More     23

6 Index     24

7 About the Author     24

**Jellyfish** live in the ocean.

5

The body of a jellyfish is called a **bell**.

bell

7

A jellyfish opens and closes
its bell to move through
the water.

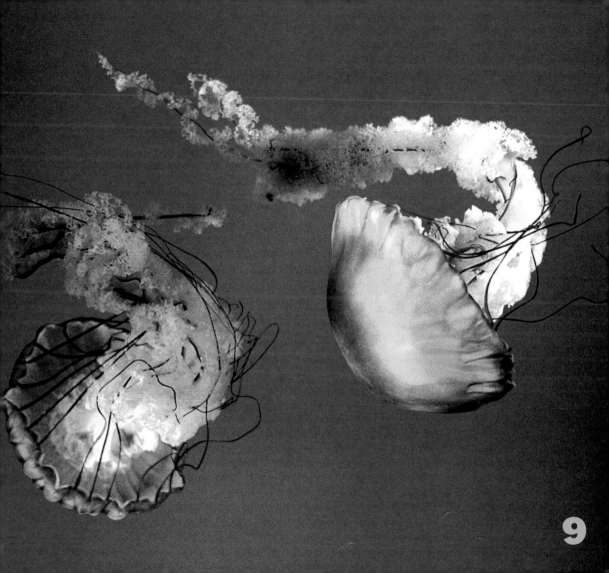

9

A jellyfish has a mouth at the bottom of its bell.

It uses its mouth to eat.

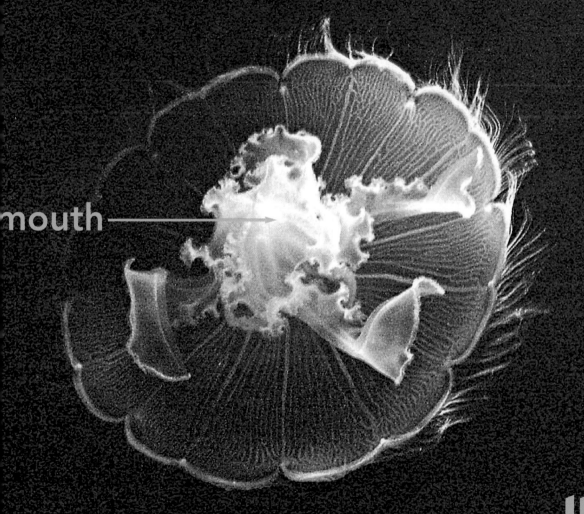

mouth

Jellyfish also have **tentacles**.

They use their tentacles to **sting** animals they want to eat.

tentacles

13

There are many kinds of jellyfish.

They can be different colors and sizes.

15

The Lion's Mane jellyfish is the largest jellyfish in the world.

Its tentacles can grow to be 200 feet long.

tentacles

Some jellyfish **glow**.

19

It is fun to learn about jellyfish.

# New Words

bell  (**bel**) the body of a jellyfish

glow  (**gloh**) to give off a steady light

jellyfish  (**jel**-ee-fish) a sea creature that
has tentacles and is soft like jelly

sting  (**sting**) to hurt with a sharp pain

tentacles  (**ten**-tuh-kuhlz) the long, flexible
limbs of certain sea creatures, such as
the jellyfish

# To Find Out More

**Books**
*Jellies: The Life of Jellyfish*
by Twig C. George
Millbrook Press, Incorporated

*Jellyfish*
by Lola M. Schaefer
Heinemann Library

**Web site**
**Enchanted Learning: Jellyfish**
http://www.EnchantedLearning.com/subjects/invertebrates/
   jellyfish/Jellyfishcoloring.shtml
Learn more about jellyfish and print out a picture of jellyfish
to color on this Web site.

# Index

bell, 6, 8, 10

colors, 14

glow, 18

Lion's Mane
  jellyfish, 16

mouth, 10

ocean, 4

sizes, 14

sting, 12

tentacles,
  12, 16

water, 8

About the Author

Lloyd G. Douglas writes children's books from his home near the Atlantic Ocean.

Content Consultant

Maria Casas, Marine Research Associate, Graduate School of Oceanography, University of Rhode Island

Reading Consultants

Kris Flynn, Coordinator, Small School District Literacy, The San Diego County Office of Education

Shelly Forys, Certified Reading Recovery Specialist, W.J. Zahnow Elementary School, Waterloo, IL

Paulette Mansell, Certified Reading Recovery Specialist, and Early Literacy Consultant, TX